FROM RED CLAY & SALT WATER

PRINCE EDWARD ISLAND & ITS PEOPLE

JOHN SYLVESTER

RAGWEED
THE ISLAND PUBLISHER

Design by:
Janet Riopelle

Printed and bound in Canada by:
D.W. Friesen

*Ragweed Press acknowledges the
generous support of the Canada
Council and the Canada/P.E.I.
Cooperation Agreement on Cultural
Development.*

Published by:
Ragweed Press
P.O. Box 2023
Charlottetown, P.E.I.
Canada C1A 7N7

Second Printing, 1997

Canadian Cataloguing in Publication Data

Sylvester, John, 1955-

From red clay & salt water

ISBN 0-921556-40-3

1. Prince Edward Island — Pictorial works.
2. Prince Edward Islanders — Interviews.*
3. Prince Edward Islanders — Portraits.*
I. Title.

FC2617.4.S95 1994   971.7'04'0222   C94-950051-8
F1047.S95 1994

For Katelyn, Alissa and Eric.

ACKNOWLEDGEMENTS

For their assistance in helping me find some of the people who appear in this book, I'm very grateful to Nancy-Marie Arsenault (for suggesting her mother), Mac Campbell, Sherrie Davidson, Harry Fraser, Kevin "Boomer" Gallant, Jim Jenkins of the Department of Fisheries and Oceans Canada, Eric MacEwen, and Ray Sark. Thanks also to Enterprise P.E.I., Tignish Fisheries Co-op, Gordon Ching, Wesley Campbell, the Chaisson family and the Arsenault family of St-Chrysostome.

Thanks to my editors at Ragweed Press, Sibyl Frei and Lynn Henry, for their encouragement and guidance.

A special thanks to my wife Dianne, for her support and understanding during a very busy time in our lives.

Above all, I would like to thank the people who gave their time, shared their experiences with me, and spoke from the heart. Without them, this book would never have been possible.

◆ ◆ ◆ ◆ ◆ ◆ ◆ ◆ ◆ ◆ ◆ ◆

CONTENTS

♦ ♦ ♦ ♦ ♦ ♦ ♦ ♦ ♦ ♦ ♦ ♦ ♦ ♦

INTRODUCTION

My discovery of Prince Edward Island began in June 1982. I knew very little about Canada's smallest province before my arrival. I'd heard about its red soil and beaches and, from Stompin' Tom Connors' song *Bud the Spud*, I knew that it was famous for growing potatoes. I also knew vaguely about a fictitious little red-haired girl named "Anne of Green Gables," the creation of Island author Lucy Maud Montgomery. And, thanks to my years of hanging around university coffee houses during the early 1970s, I knew of another famous Island author — "The People's Poet," Milton Acorn. Armed with these few scraps of knowledge, I boarded the ferry in Caribou, Nova Scotia on a fine June evening and set sail for the Island, not really knowing what to expect. When I drove off the boat in Wood Islands and joined the line of cars winding its way towards Charlottetown, through a countryside of green fields and blue coves rimmed by a red shoreline glowing orange in the evening light, I was spellbound.

Native legend explains that Prince Edward Island was formed from red clay the Great Spirit had left over after creating the Mi'kmaq people. The Great Spirit decided to fashion the clay into a crescent shape and place it in the Gulf of St. Lawrence. It would be the most beautiful place on earth, covered with lush forests, green grass and brightly coloured flowers.

The Great Spirit must have created the Island in June, for in that month it's easy to believe that it is the most beautiful place on earth. It's still my favourite time on the Island. The north shore harbours are bustling with the activity of lobster season, purple lupins line the roadsides and, in the words of Lucy Maud Montgomery, "the greenness of everything is something to steep your soul in."

I never got over that first encounter. So I moved to the Island and I've been here ever since. For a landscape photographer, it's paradise. From the greenness of June to the golds of late summer to the deep red of the fields in fall after plowing, the scene is always changing. Winter, too, has its own charm — whether it's the aftermath of an ice storm, a "silver freeze," or spotting a red fox digging for mice under the snow. There is plenty of inspiration.

Although it was landscape that first attracted me to Prince Edward Island, you can't live here long without realizing that the land, the sea and the human history are inextricably entwined. I like to call it "the living landscape" because so many people still earn their livelihood from the land and sea. They have a daily working relationship with their environment, and it's that relationship that began to intrigue me.

The Mi'kmaq, as the Island's first inhabitants, lived in harmony with the land and sea. They fished and hunted, and gathered shellfish in the incredibly rich estuaries and bays. Today these same bays continue to provide a living to shell fishers who harvest oysters, mussels, clams and quahogs. Meanwhile, lobster, once regarded as nothing better than "fertilizer," has become the mainstay of one of the few healthy fisheries remaining in Atlantic Canada.

The European settlers cleared virtually the entire Island for agriculture. And agriculture remains the number one economic activity to this day, thanks in large part to the potato industry. The province is ideally suited for growing potatoes because of its cool climate, stone-free soil and the fact that it is an island, which limits the spread of disease. That combination, along with deep water ports that are only minutes from farmers' fields, has propelled the Island into a position as one of the world's leading exporters of seed potatoes.

Together, farming and fishing have shaped the physical character of Prince Edward Island. They are also the foundation of a unique rural culture. The people you will meet in these pages feel strongly about what they do and the place where they live. At times I was moved to tears by the depth of feeling they expressed. "It's in my blood," "It runs in your veins," "He's a true-born fisherman," and "I just got imprinted on the place," are some of the phrases I heard used to describe attachments to traditions, work and place.

When I began this project in the winter of 1993, I started with the interviews. I reasoned that people would have more time in winter to stop and talk. To a certain extent, that was true. But many told me to "come back in the summer, that's when things are really happening." They were right. By springtime the pace had picked up considerably, and by mid-summer the pattern of my life began to mirror the lives of the individuals I was documenting. It

was a pattern imposed by weather and activity, and, as the summer progressed, the activities began to overlap. First it was lobster season, then haying time, Irish mossing season, harness racing during "Old Home Week," grain harvesting, oyster season, then, finally, potato harvesting time. In between, there were fiddle festivals, house parties and fairs. It all seemed squeezed into an impossibly short period of time. However, no matter how busy people were, they always made time for me, my questions and my camera. I felt privileged to be let into their lives.

In June, I joined North Lake fisher Walter Bruce and his son Scott while they hauled lobster traps in the waters off East Point. Three tides meet at that location, and even though it appeared to be a calm day, I wasn't prepared for the chop and roll of the sea. My landlubber's legs buckled under me. I was glad that Walter didn't use his father's cure for seasickness on me — a bucket of cold salt water in the face!

July was one of the wettest on record. I shared the frustrations of farmers David and Edith Ling as they tried to bring in their hay crop between downpours. When I photographed the potato harvest at Wesley and Isabel Campbell's farm later in the fall, Wesley told me that yields were down from previous years. The reason? A dry August. "Weather," says Isabel, "is second nature to everything you do in farming."

On Labour Day weekend I joined a gathering of people at Hélène Bergeron's house in Abrams Village. It was the last day of the local Acadian Festival and they had come to celebrate. Hélène's father, the acclaimed Acadian musician Eddie Arsenault, was there playing tune after rollicking tune on the fiddle. "Piling on the bois sec," he calls it. Occasionally, someone would jump out into the middle of the room to perform an impromptu step dance. It seemed to me that just about everyone there could play the fiddle or dance a "step." Some even did both at the same time! As I sat there enjoying the wonderful music, I was joined by a fiddler who had travelled halfway across the province to be at the party. He said, "This is one of the best-kept secrets on the Island."

It was difficult to stop working on this book. I kept hearing about someone else I should interview, about another subject I should include. When the last picture was taken and all the interviews finally transcribed and edited, I felt like it was only a beginning. The Island had revealed some of its secrets, but there is still much more to discover.

♦ ♦ ♦ ♦ ♦ ♦ ♦

THE
ISLAND

The coastline is our most natural environment. The coastline is pristine.

DIANE GRIFFIN, BIOLOGIST

Our soils were formed essentially under water, under oxidizing conditions, so the iron in the soil is in its ferric state, its red state. The so-called "parent" material was formed under these oxidizing conditions.

IAN MACQUARRIE, BIOLOGIST

We don't have clay soils. It's Island loam. Our soils have no clay content, so when you talk about "Island clay," it's essentially a misnomer. I've heard the expression all my life, of course, especially when referring to the "clay roads." But they're not clay.

IAN MACQUARRIE

When Cartier came here in 1534, the entire province was forested, with the exception of the sand dunes, peat bogs and salt marshes. Everything else was beautiful hardwood forest.

DIANE GRIFFIN

Much of it was cleared for agriculture and allowed to revert to quite a different sort of woodland. But if you think of, say, Strathgartney Park, if you went there three or four hundred years ago, you'd find the same species. You'd have no trouble identifying trees that were there then and now.

IAN MACQUARRIE

We've lost several things. We had moose here — they're gone. We almost certainly would have had elk. There was lynx here — that's gone. The walrus, the famous seacow, is no longer here. The black bear — the last one went out about the time of the First World War. In general we don't have any large animals.

Ian MacQuarrie

OPPOSITE: *In terms of the flowering plants, many of the ones that we find here now are so-called exotics. They were brought in by the settlers, often accidently as weeds. At a guess, thirty percent of the flowering plants that you see around now would not have been around then — the lupin is a good example.*

IAN MACQUARRIE

The wetlands probably would have been burned over a number of times, but the plant life there is much as it would have been since glaciation. When people come here they can't believe things like Malpeque Bay, for example, the quality of water and life there. Salt marshes, the bogs, sand dune systems — the nice thing about the Island is that you can get to these things in ten minutes.

IAN MACQUARRIE

Sand dunes are the most fragile of habitats on Prince Edward Island. Our sand dunes are the areas of the province where we can most get the feeling of wilderness. For instance, if you were walking out the long Blooming Point sandspit, it's very quiet. The wind and the waves, or maybe the chirping of the birds is all you would hear. I can't think of anywhere else in this province that you can get such a feeling of wilderness.

Diane Griffin

OPPOSITE: *We had a relationship with the Strait and the ocean and the Gulf. There were a lot of people here involved in the schooner trade. That sort of connection was, I think, an important part of life here. That might have been our equivalent to wilderness.*

Ian MacQuarrie

In the rest of Canada, you have the feeling that the wilderness is just behind your back. Here, of course, it isn't. There is very little left in Atlantic Canada, but we have essentially none. On the other hand, I think we've created a very attractive, almost European, type of pastoral landscape in many parts of the Island. We have a particular landscape quality now — diverse, intermingled, pastoral, often architecturally interesting — and I think that can slip away so easily.

IAN MACQUARRIE

When I was growing up there would be, say, one or two cottages and about a dozen farms, and now there seems to be hundreds of cottages and very few farms. And the farms that are there are essentially all one big field. To me that landscape is still viable, but it's not as attractive as it was. It doesn't have the diversity it had.

IAN MACQUARRIE

The whole business of the relationship between people and culture and land is so complicated. Just like a salmon imprinting on a salmon stream, you get imprinted on the land. I can recognize things here that I quite literally saw fifty years ago. That's what kind of "barnacles" you onto the landscape. The intensive knowledge of a patch of ground is a good thing.

Ian MacQuarrie

◆ ◆ ◆ ◆ ◆ ◆ ◆

THE
PEOPLE

FROM

MINEGOO

JOE LABOBE

MI'KMAQ

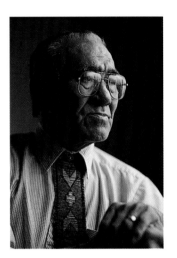

Joe Labobe

When we were growing up here on the island, we were a very closely knit family. There were quite a few of us — thirteen. We used to share a lot of our way of living. We used to have gardens and plant potatoes. Anything that we done we all worked together.

I grew up and got my education here on Lennox Island. Went up to grade eight in a day school. Then I had to quit school on account of hard times we had on the island here. It was the depression years. I had to go and help my father, help him make a better living. He used to fish and hunt. I remember Dad used to have about two or three [lobster] traps out here just for our own use. There was no abuse in fishing. It was just whatever we needed.

I helped Dad and my brother getting wood in the hard times. We used to go six or seven miles with the hand sleigh and cut wood and haul the sleigh back home with maple or whatever wood they used for making baskets. We had sort of a routine going. One day we would go to get wood for the baskets, next day we would get wood for the house, and the next day we would go hunting. It was just like that all winter. It was more for survival. There was no work at all on Lennox Island or elsewhere. It was the depression time.

We never had any doctor that would come every week. Mom was the one that used to do all the work as a doctor. She had Indian medicine. There was a lot of things that she used to cure.

*Mi'kmaq weaver
David Bernard*

My father was a weaver. He used to pound ash. They used to have a big stone tied to a wood block. They pounded the ash [on the stone] by hand with a small axe. They'd pound the stick back and forth seven or eight times and all of a sudden it would start coming apart in small strips. It's hard work.

That used to be the real source of employment for the people. They made as many as five hundred baskets in one week, mostly potato baskets. At that time, before these [mechanical] harvesters, people used to make them by the hundreds. The first time that I can remember, there was no cash involved. It was a trade. You'd go and take twenty baskets or fifty baskets to a store, they'd make up how much they're worth, and they'd give you the goods, the groceries.

They used to make axe handles here too. By golly they used to make good axe handles. You could almost use them without an axe on them. I remember my Dad used to get a bunch of them made and we'd put them in the hand sleigh, and go around to different farmers and sell them. And they used to make lobster trap hoops, and they used to make those by the thousands.

"We went way in the woods
looking for mink."

We never had any causeway here on the island. We were isolated in the spring and the fall of the year. But we had to go off the island to hunt, because there was nothing here for us except rabbits. I remember one time, it was a cold night, and the next day we started out to walk across the first overnight ice. The overnight ice is flexible. My brother was walking in front of me and he was carrying a wave and so was I. The ice was going up like a wave. We had to walk fast — if you stood still, you'd go right down. I never forgot that. So anyway, we got across [to] the other side, we walked on the edge of the valley, that's about six or seven miles, and we went way in the woods looking for mink. It was a real cold night, and we made a lean-to in the woods. We cut some boughs and put them on the bottom to make it more comfortable. We'd take turns sleeping and the other one would watch the fire. That's how we survived the night. And the next morning we went back home. We knew the ice was going to be safe. This is how we were living before the causeway was built.

When I left home here, there was no telephones, no electric. Oil lamps were used for light. But when I left in 1952, everyone here had gardens. They were sort of independent, you know.

When I got out of the service in 1967, I started snaring foxes. I went around asking different people how to set snares. Nobody gave me no satisfaction. They were getting foxes but they wouldn't tell me how they were doing it. So I said, "Okay, I'll learn myself." Whenever the first snowfall came, I would look at where they're travelling and I would mark the tree where I would put the snare. A fox has its own territory and he'll go every twenty-four hours or forty-eight hours in the same pattern. I knew that much. But setting up the snares, I didn't know anything about it. I knew a man, and he told me that the foxes have the same pattern — when they're travelling their head is down. And he used to tell me that you start winging the path with branches on each side, windrow. This is what I done, and when I caught my first fox doing that, then I knew. One morning I caught four foxes all in line and the people wondered how I was doing it. I wouldn't tell them. I wouldn't give them the satisfaction of giving them what I was doing. I did well that winter.

♦ ♦ ♦

A lot of culture is not practised anymore. It might be a bit, but it's not like when I was growing up, [although] there is people that are practising traditional values — they're drumming up here. The way we were brought up was going to church. I don't think I ever missed a Mass when I was growing up. Mom used to chase us to church if we didn't go. I never seen any of that traditional values at that time, never — although we lived more traditional.

Even though I left the reserve here when I was young, I never forgot my language. We spoke it at home, Mom and Dad, and all my brothers and sisters. My wife is an Ojibway Indian and she has a different language than mine, so our children are caught in between, where they speak English. They don't understand my language and they don't understand her language. But someday, with our grandchildren, we're going to try and teach them.

"A fox has its own territory ..."

FROM
THE
SEA

ROY COFFIN

FERRY CAPTAIN

I started in June 1961 in the Steward's Department and more or less worked my way up. I've been a captain since 1972.

You get attached to a ship. To this day I feel better about the new *Abegweit* than I do about the *Gray*. It's just because I was on the new *Abby* from day one. It's only normal if you work on it more than another one, you'll get attached to it.

Shiphandling, that's an art in itself. It's something that you only learn through experience. I was quite fortunate. I came up through the ranks, and I worked mate with other masters that had been here for a long time. You observe how they do it and you learn from what they tell you.

The technology in the navigational equipment today has really made a lot of strides. Right now we

Roy Coffin

OPPOSITE: *"The biggest challenge of sailing this route [is] the ice."*

have equipment that will give you an instant read out of latitude and longitude. In the old days you had to take sun sights to keep track of your position. Also the propulsion gear: if you go way back [when] you wanted to get your orders to the engine room, you had to ring a telegraph, and the engineer down below he would hear that order. Sometimes it would get mixed up between the bridge and the engine room. So you can imagine what happens there. Now it's all bridge-controlled.

The biggest challenge of sailing this route [is] the ice. We're dealing with ice here from mid-January right through to the end of March, and sometimes almost the middle of April. It's not really the thickness that creates the problem, it's the pressure that gets on it. That's why if they compare ice here to ice somewhere else where there is not the current, it doesn't really have the same effect, because it's the wind effect and the currents. We know very well that if we don't allow for the movement of the ice, you'd never get docked, you'd never get into the harbour. You have to know what the ice is doing and allow for that.

[One time,] it had blown north-west for about three days. The Strait was jammed full of ice and it wasn't moving at all, but there was tremendous pressure on it. We were out here about three miles off Borden on the *John Hamilton Gray* and we got jammed. We couldn't go ahead and we couldn't go astern. How we eventually ended up getting out — the old *Abegweit* left Borden and made her way out towards us. When she got about three or four ship lengths away from us, there was a sound like a shot out of a cannon, like an explosion. The ice let go and our stern swung right around — pretty near ninety degrees — toward the *Abby.* But at least we were clear and we finally worked our way in.

I forget what year it was that the ice came in over the shoal at Cape Tormentine, up over the pier and out over the railway tracks and the road. There was mountains of ice, they had to get a front-end loader to clear it away. There were railway cars on the siding. It came all over top of them and it took two or three days to move all the ice so they could get those flat cars out of there. I would never have believed it if I hadn't seen it, that the ice could do that. There was a wooden seawall on the top of the pier and it just splintered that all over onto the roadway.

I would like for the people who are designing the [Northumberland Strait] bridge and constructing it to see something like that. Then I think they would have more respect for the ice.

CLIVE BRUCE

LOBSTER FISHER

I grew up in East Baltic. I was seventeen when I started fishing at Red Point Beach. There was about twenty of us there. [We'd] haul all the boats up on the beach at night and launch them all in the morning and go fishing. I started with an older man and his son. The old fella was left-handed and the young fella was right-handed. I had to learn to split fish. So when the old fella dropped his knife, I learned left-handed and when the young fella dropped his knife I learned right-handed. I could split both ways. We'd dress them [the fish] down on the sand. Then we'd carry them all up to the fish house and salt them there.

We all lived in shacks along the shore. We left home Sunday evening. We had to walk to the shore — it was about three miles. I'd take a basket of grub with me, bread and salt meat. My mother used to take part of a pig and fry it all up and put it in a crock and [put] salt on the top in a cloth so it wouldn't spoil. That's the way we got our

Clive Bruce

meat. Well, then, you couldn't buy canned milk. What we used to take was water with molasses in it. Just take a cup of cold water and for to give it sweetener, put a little molasses in it. The only butter we had was made in a crock. Not very often we cooked potatoes, but we used to cut out an awful lot of fish tongues and cheeks, and fry them up in lard or butter. And that's the way we lived. It was a rough living, but it was a good healthy living.

I remember Johnny. His father used to take him out and he'd have to turn around and take him in. He come over and said "Clive, Dad won't take me. Will you take me?" I said, "Yes I'll take you, but remember I'm not coming to shore with you." We got half way out, he says, "I'm getting sick." He was there with his head down, turning inside out. I reached over and got a half bucket of water. I give it to him right in the face. I soaked him. I said, "Now you sit there and think about everything nice you ever learned. Whistle. You'll be all right in a few minutes." "It won't make me sick?" I said, "No, if you sit with your face to the wind, you'll be all right in no time." So the first net I picked off the boat, I looked beside me and there was Johnny up helping me. He was never sick afterwards. You give a fella a start like that, it's settling his nerves. I had a lot of young fellas fish for me and the first day or two they were getting sick. So when I felt they were getting good and sick I gave them a good dish of water. Course it made them good and mad. It's a wonder they didn't fire me overboard. But it cured them.

They got better traps today than we had. They got these great "boxcar" traps. The poor lobster would sooner crawl into it than go around it, that's what I figure. I'd say if fisheries don't clamp down on the size of the traps, they're going to clean 'er. 'Cause each year they're making them bigger.

I was fishing for sixty-four, sixty-five years. It was an independent life, you were your own boss. If I was a young man today, I'd go back to sea again.

OPPOSITE: *"It was an independent life."*

Walter Bruce

Lobster Fisher

"I've seen a lot of changes …"

I started with my father, fishing with him two years. This'll be thirty-one on my own. I was fifteen when I went with him. I guess there was a place there, and I liked it, and that's why I got into it. I have three brothers and they're all fishing, and two nephews, they're fishing now.

I've seen a lot of major changes myself. I started in an open boat, a stick for steering. And a gas engine and a truck transmission and an old capstan for a trap hauler. My sounder was a lead of twine, a reel that you dropped down, and a compass. That was all the navigation equipment that you had, and you made do with that. I always found my gear and I always made it to shore. Today you have a fibreglass boat with an oil stove, bunks, Loran, radar, depth finders, marine navigation, just about everything you want. I've gone from almost the days of rowing to everything that an ocean-going ship has aboard. You still have to do the physical work. We have a trap hauler that pulls the rope in so you don't have to stand there and go hand over hand. You still got to physically set it down, take the fish out, bait it. And you still got to be out there in the rough weather, so that part hasn't changed.

When I started first, we fished a lot of traps. I fished as high as eleven hundred traps. The average was around eight hundred or nine hundred per boat. There was no trap limit. We came to realize all we were doing was working for the supply companies. You know, buying gear and rope and working ourselves to death. We thought a trap limit was the way to go. We had an association then and went looking for a trap limit and a licence freeze. So the government gave us the trap limit, but they didn't give us the licence freeze. So the licence out there at the [North] Lake went from forty-five up to the hundred figure. Then they put the licence freeze on. Basically

Walter Bruce

what happened [is] we took our traps out of the water, moved over and made room for other people.

We used to go into groundfish, then tuna, then back to groundfish to finish the season. But with the depletion of the groundfish stocks now, that's almost a sport fishery. We still chase tuna. Now we go down as far as Shelburne chasing tuna. That's over one hundred and twelve miles offshore. Even twenty years ago you wouldn't dream of doing that unless you had a big steel dragger or ocean freighter or something. But you're driven to those things now, because of the lack of fish on your own doorstep.

"Now there's a joke going around that the cod are so small the lobsters are eating them!"

A lot of people say: the fish, the fishermen destroyed them. Well, they did destroy the small ones when they were highgrading, especially the big boats. The big companies were more to blame. But who issued the quotas? The in-shore fishermen in Newfoundland — the same here in the Gulf — [said] that the stocks were going into trouble. It turns out the in-shore guy, the independent fella that was on the shore, he turned out to be right. It's sad.

It used to be when I started first, you'd look over the side of the boat in June and you'd see the big cod swimming there on a nice day catching the small lobsters as you fired them over. Now there's a joke going around that the cod are so small the lobsters are eating them!

◆ ◆ ◆ ◆ ◆ ◆ ◆ ◆ ◆ ◆ ◆ ◆

JEAN ARSENAULT

FISH PLANT WORKER

I always worked at the plant. It used to be that it was only the family that could work there. If the father was a fisherman then the wife could go in, or the daughter and the son. But it's not like that anymore, it's whoever comes first.

When I was fourteen, I started working at the plant. In those days you didn't go to school because you couldn't afford to go to school. You had to go out and work. I started working in North Cape. We'd leave Sunday afternoon and we'd work 'til Saturday five o'clock, six o'clock, and we'd go home, get a change of clothes, and there were not too many clothes I'll tell you either, and then go back for the next week, and stay at an outside camp. It was the same season then — May 'til the last of June. Then they'd open again in August 'til October the tenth. We'd work the month of July putting up mackerel, chicken haddie or blueberries, if we could find enough blueberries to put up, things like that. It was what everyone did.

Jean Arsenault

It was hard work compared to what it is now. There were no machines like there is now. That's what took all the work from the workers, too many machines. Cracking claws was the hardest, cause they didn't have the proper knives, like the knives they have today. And the lobsters then were not like the lobsters they have today. They were bigger lobsters, and the bigger the lobster the harder the shell. It wasn't fun, let me tell you. We were glad when the season was over.

"You put the meat in the can just as quick as it comes in."

The hardest it is [now], and there is a lot of people that complain about that — is the cement [floor]. You're standing on it and the cold water runs all the time. We're in a building, no windows, no fresh air at all. We're in there two hours, with the machines, all that racket. Then there's fumes that comes from the machines, and sometimes the freezer backfires and you get this strong smell of ammonia. There's no windows, so they can't let that out. That was the biggest mistake they ever made. In the old plant we had a window every four feet. And if we got warm or if we wanted some fresh air, we opened up the window. They took the windows out cause they said the people spent too much time looking out the window. So they turned that around and built a plant with no windows at all.

I worked all over the plant [in Tignish]. These last seven years I been at the packing table because I couldn't hack the cold water, I couldn't hack the cracking, it was just too much for me. So I went to the packing table and I been there ever since. At the packing table you don't get no water. It's just the meat, and you put the meat in the can just as quick as it comes in. There's no sitting, everybody stands.

I love the plant, I loved working. It's the people, eh. We all know everybody. Everybody gets along good. There's no fighting. Everybody's always glad to see this one, to see that one. In the morning, we used to stand outside before the bell would ring, see how much stories we could get, like what happened the night before. Things like that. Gossip, that's the word.

I worked at the salt fish right until the twenty-third of January, when I took sick. I loved working.

I've sold my uniforms, my hats, I only got my boots to go. I might save my boots for a souvenir, go fishing trout.

"I loved the plant, I loved working. It's the people, eh."

JOEY PERRY

IRISH MOSS HARVESTER

I hauled moss for years from Rustico. We'd start there early in the spring. There'd still be ice in the water. Then we hauled there late, late, late in the fall. One time the whole families were into it. The wife, the husband, the kids, everybody. It was a good living. Years ago you'd think nothing of paying fifteen hundred, eighteen hundred dollars for an old work horse to go mossing. I know, I done it. You'd get a new truck every second year. One time the moss was so good here that the lobster fishermen — lobsters weren't that plentiful at that time — they'd fish maybe four to six weeks. They'd haul their gear in and they'd go rake moss for the rest of the fall.

There's two different ways that we moss. First of all, you go out and rake it. We all have rakes on the boats. Some haul it aboard with a winch. Other lads like meself, we just rake by hand — we're alone in the boat. When we rake by hand, we bring one rake up at a time with a hydraulic hauler. Any calm day we're out there raking. We don't get it all when we haul the rakes in, eh, just so much falls off the rakes. That'll all go back to the bottom. The least little storm, that'll all wash ashore. That's when we harvest it on the shore. That's when we used to use the horses.

Joey Perry

"We bring one rake up at a time with a hydraulic raker."

You can go down to Naufrage, and back forty years ago there was tons of Irish moss there. You couldn't haul it away. Then all of a sudden these other weeds started to take over until there was completely no Irish moss. Go down to Rustico, the same way. We used to haul moss from Rustico that tested eighty, eighty-five percent moss. You go down to Rustico today, there's no way you could find a load of moss that could test five percent. And you take Tignish side, it's the same way out there. We used to moss all out along Kildare, beautiful moss. Other weeds took over. Just like it was working right around the Island.

"That's what a fella misses the most of all, is being on the shore."

They used to dry the moss and keep it and sell it all winter. You'd have a room in the house. Over home we used to have the basement. In the fall of the year we'd fill that. A man used to come around, maybe on Fridays, and you'd have maybe three or four bags of moss and he'd buy that from you. That was your money for groceries and whatever you were going to need. Yeah, there was nothing else. There was fishing but there was no money to be made fishing, not like it is today, and there was no such thing as "unemployment" [insurance].

There's only one horse left in Miminegash here now. Ten years ago there'd have been fifty or sixty, maybe more. Everybody had a horse, some of them had two, some of them had three. But the last couple of years everybody got out of it. I got rid of mine last fall. It's a shame eh, all of them nice big horses, just no use for them anymore.

There was a lot of laughs and a lot of fun along that shore. Along the shore everybody helped everybody else. That's what a fella misses the most of all, is being on the shore.

SUPER DENNIS

OYSTER FISHER

I worked with a couple of old fellas that were brought up here down at the shore. I'm fifty-one, and I think the first time I went picking oysters I was seven. It wasn't at all steady. You couldn't get into it far enough at that time to make any money. You could never support a family. You can now, it's going up every year.

It's a business now. That's all I do, is fish. I don't do anything else, just oysters and quahogs. In those days you couldn't sell quahogs either — you couldn't give them away. We used to curse them and bounce them off the boards. Now the quahogs is about on par with the oysters or, price-wise, they may be even a little better.

We fish when the tide starts to go out. We fish it all the way out and all the way back in. Most dories have twelve-foot, ten-foot, eight-foot and six-foot tongs, so they'll start off with the tens and work down to the eights and down to the sixes as the tide drops. They'll

"Second to none."

work the sixes all the time the tide's down. Then when it starts up and they get too short on the sixes, then they go back to the eights and they go back to the tens. Then you got a box that's only half full and you want to get it full, so you grab the twelves and fill it and go home. That's usually six or seven hours a day. Some days you can get longer hours than that.

For years these fellas here, and I did it too, just went out and got what you could get. You weren't concerned whether the water was blue or if it was brown or if it was yellow or what it was. You got what you could get and you went home, and you sold it and that was it.

Not any more. Every one of these guys that's running up and down the river there with them dories know that if they screw up something in this water, they're cutting their own throat. The fishermen all got together and we fight pretty hard. If there's something going on up and down the river that's going to cause us any problems, they'll just go clean up in arms over it. Because they've put so many hours, so many cold days out here, trying to bring this stuff back so that we could have a fishery. It is aquaculture in a way. We're making sure there is going to be something there to harvest next year. Some people look at those [mud flats] and just see mud, but to me it's my farm. We're farmers. That's exactly what we are.

We all work together. It would be nothing to come in here in the fall of the year and see seven guys in here, getting their oysters all packed. Each fella comes in and four or five grab his oysters and get things loaded.

OPPOSITE: *Super Dennis*

49

"We all work together."

Those fellas right there [oysters] are second to none in the world, because of the taste. It's all in the taste. They're natural, you can eat them any time of year. One of the things is that the water's cold, and it's clean. We don't have any heavy industry in P.E.I. We got no car manufacturing plants, no battery acid plants.

You'd be surprised how many people would spend an hour opening one of those oysters just to get one. The taste is something unreal.

FROM

THE

LAND

H.B. WILLIS

POTATO FARMER

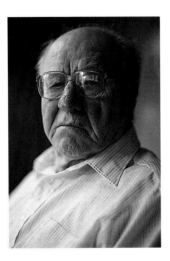

H.B. Willis

During the war, I started out with "truck garden" vegetables on this land here. I conveyed them to Charlottetown with a horse and wagon to peddle them door-to-door . Many customers were very, very glad to get such deliveries and service. They paid well for it. It started me out in life and I kept buying land. And when the war come to an end I figured I would have to get into something else. So I got into the commercial end of growing potatoes. It was the days when horse equipment was going out of style rapidly and tractors were coming into style. So I converted into the tractor age, and went on from there, bought some land around me here and started growing potatoes.

[I asked myself] what am I going to do with these potatoes after I grow them? So I went out in the outside world and explored the market to see what I could accomplish. I went to the United States and made some connections there. That built up, and built up, and from there I went down into the foreign fields to see what I could develop.

Understanding the climatic conditions that you had to compete against was one of the biggest things to learn. The temperature in Venezuela at the unloading port was so hot [that] taking the potatoes right from the very cold ship and landing them in that extreme heat in that country was impossible. It was just like putting snow out in the middle of July here — it won't last long. We lost a shipload of potatoes down there one year. I was down there, discouraged, you'd better believe it. Man alive, I didn't know which way to turn — whether to jump over the wharf or what to do. They were a little immature when they went into the ship. The immaturity of them here together with the shock of the extreme cold and the extreme heat, that's when they melted. They melted like snow. So we worked on it from one ship to another and finally we got to the remedy of adjusting the temperature of the ship en route to within about five or ten degrees of the domestic temperature in that port.

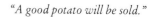

You've got to be what we call a "horse trader" to be in the potato business. You got to be able to think pretty quick and act very quickly. It's a commodity that only lasts so long. It's a hell of a business.

A good potato will be sold. There is a buyer for it every day. You don't have to sell it, it will sell itself. I like them boiled in the jacket, a little pure butter on them when you open them up. If you can't make a meal of that, you're not that hungry.

ISABEL CAMPBELL

FARMER

I grew up on a small farm. My father was a carpenter. He did both things, farming and carpentry work. It was common years ago on your smaller farms.

When my husband, Wes, and I got married, almost every home down the road was occupied by a bona fide farmer, say twelve to fifteen farms. Today, there's four actually farming.

People think you're well off, but it's all tied up in the farm. The first little bit of profit you get, you invest it back into the farm to update your machinery and repair buildings. Since there was no retirement plan for the older generation, they couldn't really get off the farm when they wanted. That's been traditional, that's how farms survived. Every member of the family couldn't be paid for their work — the true cost of producing food has always been invisible.

Up until the eighties you could have a fairly comfortable living farming full-time. Now we've gone full circle and people are taking an off-farm job for the privilege of farming.

It seemed that it didn't matter how hard you worked in the eighties, the prices kept skyrocketing. Some people expanded their operations, and bought land, in order to start paying for the high cost of machinery. It became a vicious circle. It only makes the situation ripe for corporate takeover — not only here but really worldwide. Farms can only stand so much pressure.

Isabel and Wesley Campbell

Women with careers certainly help to keep a farm. It's kind of an accepted way of life. But in many instances the women pretty well have a triple workload because they're still needed on the farm and in the house.

On the farm the women usually do the gardening, the housework, the painting or sewing, and they help outside. That's been my observation. It doesn't matter how busy you are in the house, the farm has to take priority. If you're needed, you're needed.

It was really nice when the children were little. I remember the summer evenings when we would be out until dark working. The children wouldn't be in bed as early, and at three, four and five years, they didn't have to be in school. That was just a wonderful, favourite time. But then they went to school and they'd get off the bus to find me in the garden. They'd run to see what Dad was doing. They were so excited. There was always so much to talk about. Life was never dull.

"It doesn't matter how busy you are in the house, the farm has to take priority."

Weather is second nature to everything you do in farming. When it's sleet and snow, it impacts on the farm. There could be frozen pipes in the barn, and the weather did that. But when the south wind comes in the spring it's just, to me, sheer joy to have a nice warm south wind coming in. We hear the crickets, we see the steam rising from the land. And when you hear a far-off tractor somewhere, you know that their land's drier and they're already on it. It's putting a garden in, seeing new life, new growth, and watching everything that happens on the farm.

I love farmers as a group of people. I just have a tremendous compassion for them. People can't really understand everything about their life unless they've farmed alongside them. You're an amateur vet, a mechanic, a jack of all trades, a community person, a support person, a manager. You're everything. You just do the best you can and sometimes it's not enough.

"In the spring ... we see the steam rising from the land."

◆ ◆ ◆ ◆ ◆ ◆ ◆ ◆ ◆ ◆ ◆ ◆ ◆

DAVID & EDITH LING

ECOLOGICAL FARMERS

DAVID: I farmed all my life, ever since I was able to walk. Grew up on a tractor almost. We purchased this farm here in 1967. [In] 1970 we got married and moved up here. The first five years I was a dependent, Edith worked at the Department of Agriculture.

Back in the mid-seventies, when Edith had just quit her job, I was brainwashed to the point that I believed I had to grow two hundred acres of potatoes to make a living. Why would I, or anybody in their right mind, want to go and get themselves into a half-million dollar debt just to grow two hundred acres of potatoes? That's what Edith said: "Look if you're going to go that route, I'll go back to work." We were farming at that time two hundred and fifty acres, and we cut back to less than half that in acreage. It was pretty hard to think that you could make a living by cutting back when everyone else was going ahead. It just seemed like it was drilled into you, you had to get bigger.

It was the best thing we ever did. We're still just as busy as we were in those times but we don't have the financial overhead. We're making only a minimum amount of return on our investment. But we're still far better off than the majority of farmers are today. They're losing their equity. I still have a strong feeling that you can make an income on a small acreage. You don't need hundreds of acres.

David and Edith Ling

"I farmed all my life ..."

After three or four years, our yields were back up. They never got up to the high rates that we had been getting before, but still had an average yield that was about the same as we had before we used high inputs of fertilizer. But our soil was starting to produce an awful lot more earthworms. The soil was a good aggregate, more crumbly. And another thing I found was that it took an awful lot less horsepower to work the same implement. After five years I could really see a big change. The soil was improving. It did take, I'd say, five years to turn around. It's the same as a drug addict, you've got to detoxify the soil. It just doesn't happen overnight.

DAVID: I was farming the same way as a majority of farmers are today. We were using a fair number of chemicals then and we were constantly increasing the amount up to 1985, when I changed over to ecological farming. Our yields dropped off at least twenty-five percent. But then at the end of the year our income was the same. So we didn't really lose.

The last two years we do sell all our beef locally, in a custom trade. We're not getting really much of a premium but we're getting what's in it. Every customer we have remarks about the flavour of the meat, the tenderness. It's the same with hogs and nearly everyone remarks about the quality of the meat.

OPPOSITE: *"I still have a strong feeling that you can make an income on a small acreage."*

EDITH: I think it's a really good place to bring up children, on the farm. They get to learn about life in the happy times, and they see death. The family is closer, there is no doubt about that. And if you want to take a day off, you just plan your work and do it. There's a lot of benefits.

"The family is closer ..."

FROM
"AWAY"

MORLEY & LYNDA PINSENT

" COME FROM AWAY "

LYNDA: It wasn't a reasoned decision [to come to the Island]. We had been looking for land on the west coast for a couple of years. We took about three or four months coming across Canada. So we had a VW van and three kids and a dog that started out as a little puppy and ended up the size of a St. Bernard. We came over [to the Island] and the family kind of revolted. We were just tired of travelling. We found a big house to live in.

MORLEY: A big old abandoned farmhouse. We were surprised by the — simplicity is not the right word — almost a naivety in taking face value in people.

LYNDA: This older couple had this house that was all furnished and they didn't know who we were, whether we could pay the rent or anything. And they just accepted us. They had never gone on a holiday, and they went to Florida and had us look after their farm for them and feed their cattle and everything. They'd known us a couple of months.

MORLEY: And we're still good friends.

LYNDA: We lived over in the Baltic for that first winter. Moved here [Granville} and lived in tents that summer we built the house. Everybody in the entire community had to come have a look, I think. And then we had the hiking trail going through our property, too. There was a lot of hiking that summer! Some of them kept us alive. Several years later we found out that they had bets in North Granville as to how long we would last. I think probably the older farmers were much more accepting than the younger people, even our age or younger, would have been.

Morley Pinsent

Lynda Pinsent

MORLEY: Things go on in rural communities that wouldn't be tolerated in very many other societies anywhere. You can be different but because you're sort of a known entity, that's accepted. The first phone line came through here in 1962, 1963. There was no pavement. It was essentially quite a closed community. And there were people that were a pain, and there were nice people. But they all had to tolerate each other because you didn't have any other choice. That toleration spilled over to a lot of people like us coming from away.

"It's a very comfortable kind of place."

MORLEY: It's a very comfortable kind of place, particularly rurally. It's a very egalitarian place in a lot of ways. There's not very many wealthy people here, but there are a lot of people who are just getting by. You're all sort of partners in depression to some degree. That's very much a part of the Island way of life. The only people that have one job are the people that live in the city and go to the same job. In the country there are very rarely people that do one thing. They usually do a number of things to cobble a life together. Their vocations and avocations get all cluttered up together. Actually I really enjoy that. I think we twigged to that fairly early. It was a nice, rewarding way to make a living.

It would certainly be fair to say that native Islanders have shaped and altered our opinions to some degree. We've become much less strident, I guess. We never did have a missionary zeal, even though we were very different. When you become involved in a community in any way, you very rapidly become indebted, to the point where you're almost committed to living there for the rest of your life to pay off your debts. Not in dollars but in favours.

FROM
SKILLED
HANDS

◆　◆　◆　◆　◆　◆　◆　◆　◆　◆　◆　◆　◆　◆　◆

MALCOLM STANLEY

POTTER

Christine and I came to P.E.I. in September 1975. I had been apprenticing in a studio in New Brunswick. She had just finished up at the craft school in Fredericton. So when we came here we were a potter and weaver combination, part of that sort of "back to the land" attitude. We wanted to live that bohemian lifestyle, we really weren't into making money. It sounds so naive when I think about it now.

I think a lot of locals thought we were just a couple of crazy kids going through some sort of phase with this pottery business. But I found the older people in P.E.I. seemed to identify with that hippie generation better than the people that were closer to our age. And a lot of them could remember using pottery in everyday life back in the early part of this century, before everybody got into plastic and Tupperware. So they sort of understood what it was all about.

When Christine and I first came here we were more interested in the lifestyle than the business. And

Malcolm Stanley

then in the eighties we got very caught up in the business and sort of lost sight of why we were doing this in the first place. In the summertime I was running around being a businessman. We were open to all hours of the night up there, and I'd come home and the kids would already be asleep, and you'd get up in the morning and go again. It was fun for a few years, but when I stopped enjoying it, then I realized it wasn't what I wanted after all.

It's funny, you know. [In the summer,] people will come in and they say, "Oh boy, we really admire your laid-back lifestyle." And anybody that's involved in the handcraft business or the tourist business, or even farming or fishing, that's the busy time of year. You want to see laid back, you come back in February. We're friggin' catatonic. I like to portray that relaxed feeling; meanwhile, I'm thinking about all the coffee mugs I have [to do] in the next few weeks. You try not to let those daily annoyances creep into your conversations with the tourists. You say, "Come on out and see my ladyslipper."

I have a few scenes that I can recreate [in my work]. The nighttime scenes have really come along. I use the full moon, and I get a nice effect. Back in the early eighties when I first moved out here, I started going out cross-country skiing under the moonlight — that sort of thing just sort of creeps in. But it wasn't a real conscious decision. It was sort of a subconscious thing.

"I started going out cross-country skiing under the moonlight."

A lot of people say, "Why don't you export your work to the shops in Toronto? You could be a lot better known. How come I can't find your work in Montreal?" There's only so much pottery I can make. It's just not my style really. A lot of people think that to really make it in the pottery business, you've got to get your work to the big cities. I like to say my work is exclusive to P.E.I.

◆　◆　◆　◆　◆　◆　◆　◆　◆　◆　◆　◆　◆　◆

HILDA WOOLNOUGH

ARTIST

I came here twenty-five years ago at least. I think my first reaction was the reaction I always have every time I go across on the boat, because I love the boat trip. It gave me such a thrill. To me it looked like a sort of gigantic quilt. That was my first thought: how wonderful to live in a place like this. To go to your home, you go across in the boat. The waves and the sea and the sky — that is part of your going-home experience. I always feel like that.

Of course, where I live is very important. I see what's important

Hilda Woolnough

to me every time I look out the window. It affects the way I see forms, it affects the weights and balances and contrasts. They're all in all the work I do, I think. There's definitely a difference between an artist like myself who lives in an agrarian area, or who lives in the woods like I do, and the work of an artist who lives dead centre in Toronto, surrounded by cement. If you look at the work that comes from artists that live in agrarian areas, it's much more organic, much more rounded. So I think you are definitely influenced.

I like the sort of light you get when it's reflecting off the sea and all the things that happen there. I like the smell of it. It smells totally different than anything inland. And there's a lot more choice here, because you've got every sort of thing — you've got your sea creatures and your sea life and your sea forms. And then you have your landforms, and you have your skyforms, and you have your waterforms. You have all the forms you could possibly want, from my point of view.

There are times when you get up in the morning and you see all the grass is covered by these fine spider webs. And when a certain light hits them, they've all got dew on them. All the spinners have been at work. Just for that moment or two, that half an hour, there they are. They're visible to the eye, the human eye, then after that they're not. They dry out or get broken. That's why I live here, because of that magic.

Sometimes, towards the end of the year, actually about September, October, in the evening, there's a way that the sun has of going down, and it gets squashed somehow. And when you look away from the sun in the other direction you have this intense light, which is quite extraordinary. And the colour so vivid that you cannot believe it. It's almost like you're going in a tunnel of vivid colour. I've never seen that anywhere else but here. I don't really understand it. You get this sort of squished effect, that light is being squished in some extraordinary way. You go along and see, for instance, a yellow farmhouse on top of a hill, and you just cannot believe it — it's so stunning, the colour. And sometimes the sky is a deep vivid blue, dark blue. You can't exaggerate enough about the colour here, in my opinion.

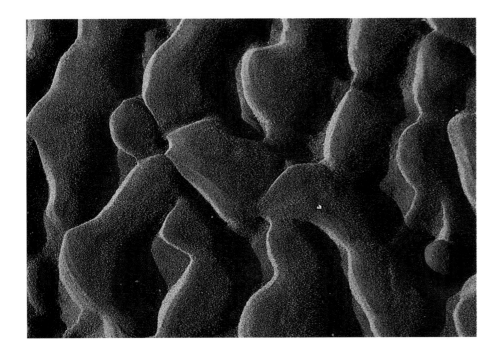

Even in the winter when the snow comes down, the colours are just stunning because you have all these blue and purple shadows in the snow. I go out here where the old orchard is and when the full moon comes up it's just like a batik on snow. And you can't believe that anything so beautiful can exist.

One time when I first came here, I was wandering around through the woods by the stream. It was early in the spring and you could see these layers of earth. And I said out loud, "That's what it's all about." And I suddenly realized about layering, about the earth and how it's formed, and we're all part of it, and this is the residue of many, many, many organic forms. That's what the earth is. It's a very comforting idea. You can see these layers, and understand the continuity of life, and that you are part of it. It's a continuum.

All these things affect the work that I do. Every single thing. Even though I'm not a realist, these sort of things creep into the work that I do. I do actually have a degree in painting, but I don't paint. I mostly work as a graphic artist — mixed media on paper mostly.

If you have any eyes whatsoever, you cannot but be totally fascinated by what is going on here. I find actually that you have to rest your eyes here. I think that if you're visually trained here, it's like the experience that you have of going into many, many galleries in one day. There's a point where you can't look any more, you can't see any more, and you're not even looking really. And I think that's true here. There's so much visual information. For artists it's wonderful.

OPPOSITE: "The colour so vivid that you cannot believe it."

RUTH PAYNTER

QUILTER

My mother quilted, and my mother hooked, and my mother sewed, and my mother did all the things that a farm woman did in her day, and didn't have a great deal of time to concentrate on any one special thing. I had an aunt that was a dressmaker and she encouraged me. It just seemed as if I always wanted to sew things together.

I didn't do any really fancy quilts until I sort of retired from farming and from my other line of handcraft. Up until then I had only made quilts, the type of quilts that everyone needed, the heavy type quilts for warmth, more than for style. You'd make them up in a hurry. I never settled down to do tiny little stitches 'til after I retired. So that only goes back about twenty years. I soon found that I wasn't just satisfied with the regular patterns. I wanted to try something original on my own. I enjoyed that part of it very much.

My quilts are different. I sort of do it as I go. I don't make too many sketches, just roughly. When

Ruth Paynter

I get my colours all sorted out, I cut a piece about the size I want. You get the feel for it as you go along through your material. I'm a little bit old-fashioned and I always save things, so I have quite a stock of material. Some of it is pretty antique looking, according to today's standards. But again, when I get into doing scenery, that's when I get into some of my old material. You wouldn't put them in an ordinary quilt, but

you'd like them as a tree or you'd like them in a little corner someplace, or little shrub or something like that. A lot of my material, if some of the modern quilters saw it, they'd throw it out, but I just hang on to it.

We have six great grandsons and one great granddaughter. I'd rather give a quilt to someone like that, who I know will appreciate it, than to put it in a shop and sell it. I wouldn't sell "Memories of the Old Home Place" because there's too much family in it. But the problem is, with two sons and one daughter, who do you give it to? As far as making a scenery quilt, taking an order and making a scenery quilt and charging somebody for the time you put in it, well, you'd scare them if you told them all the time you spent on it. But if I know a person is going to appreciate it, then I don't mind. That's my strongest feeling about my quilts.

Some people are more inclined to save something just to have it to look at and others are inclined to put it out and use it and get the good of it every day. I haven't decided yet which is the better way of livin' really — I'm inclined to save things myself!

"I used my quilt making as a way of showing my love ... of nature."

I like to think that I used my quilt making as a way of showing my love for Prince Edward Island and my love of nature. I see beauty — beauty everywhere I look. Now that's the Southwest river down there, and it's frozen over right now. But I can't wait for the spring to come, and every day it's a different colour. When the sky is dark, the water's dark. And when the sky is bright, some days you can see the shadows from the trees on the other side there reflecting in the water. It changes every day. And the trees here at Woodleigh — I just have to walk across there a short distance and I'm right in the midst of their gardens. Flowers and shrubs and birds flying around. It's heaven on earth, that's what it is.

FROM

THE

HEART

EMMETT BERNARD

HARNESS RACING

I've been around horses all my life. I started home on the farm, we had horses on the farm. The first horse I ever owned as a driver, I was about fourteen years old and I bought a horse that another fella had, and we started to race on the ice down in New Glasgow. That's the reason I bought him, for to go ice racing. That was the big thing. The Charlottetown Victoria Driving Club — we all would join it, then we'd ship the horses over by railroad to Dartmouth and we'd race on Banook Lake in Dartmouth.

Back when I started race horses I got all the old rangatangas and everything in the world, and that's how I got the name "Cowboy." I drove every bad horse that anybody else wouldn't drive. They'd say, "Ask the Cowboy, he'll drive them." Those horses

OPPOSITE: *"You can go down any road on the Island and you're going to run into horses."*

that stick in their toes and make dirty breaks, I got them. That's how I built up my reputation. I had as many as seventeen horses in my stable at once. We raced them right from here sometimes. In the wintertime, we'd take them home here and stable them and we'd jog them on the side of the road. I started with the old work horses and I caught on from there, and I've been near the next best at the track all my life. I drove as many as six dashes a night.

A lot of good horses come off these little tracks. It takes the little outside tracks to make the wheel go round. You can go down any road on this Island and you're going to run into horses. I don't care where you go, everybody's got a horse, some kind of horse — a saddle horse, a show horse, or a jumping horse, whatever he may be. We have one of the fastest bunch of horses in the Maritimes, here on the Island.

You've got to have a good horse, but if you don't have luck it doesn't matter what kind of horse you got. Once you move behind that gate, everything leaves you, you forget all about your troubles and to the front you try to go. They'll all come home for Old Home Week. You get wore out, but you stay there, eh. You don't seem to want to leave. Afraid you'll miss something I guess …

Ah, there's something about a horse. I don't know, it's worse than liquor, I'll tell you that. You get addicted to it, you can't get away from it. I've tried to get away from it now for three or four years. "That's it ," I said, "I'm through." Next thing I gone to the sale and bought another horse.

ALBERT BERNARD

HARNESS RACING

Prince Edward Island is a rural province, the people are rural people. If you didn't own a horse, your neighbour did. You went to the races to see your neighbour's horse race. That is the way it's been on Prince Edward Island as long as I can remember.

On the track you forget about your neighbour, your friend, your cousin or whatever. You're out there to win the race. Some of them will hold a grudge for a day or two, but not most of them. You get off the track and laugh about it: "I'll get you next time, you sucker." They get over it. Ninety percent have known one another from when they were kids, they were raised here.

[I've had] quite a few broken bones, steel metal in that arm, screws, plates, one of these wrists has been broken once or twice, ankle a couple of times. I've driven with casts on my hands, casts

Albert and Emmett Bernard

on my ankles. As soon as I'm able to go, I go again. Even if you have a bad spill, you get back on and go. You blank that out. As soon as you go behind the starting gate next time out, you're concentrating on that race, not on the accident you had twenty minutes ago, or two weeks or two months. You don't even think of them.

*"It's just a love for an animal
and the thrill of racing them."*

There's people think we put on
the greatest show there is in horse
racing during Old Home Week.
Even the top driver from Ontario
that won it last year, he come
down, drove a horse and couldn't
believe it. He said, "I've drove in
million dollar races that haven't
had the hype that this thing has!"

It's a show. It's a build up for the
whole week, and the climax comes
with this great presentation of
this race. Horses racing have to

qualify to get in it. The Gold Cup
and Saucer girls, the parade —
everything is geared to Gold Cup
and Saucer. It finally comes down
to the big race. And then the
presentation: the lights go out, the
singing of the Island hymn. It's
quite a feeling sitting in that bike
and you come up the stretch, the
lights go out, about eight or ten
thousand people here. We do well
to get eight hundred the next
night out!

"It's something that just gets into your blood."

It's something that just gets into your blood. You ask anyone who's in the horse business, once you get into it, it's a hard thing to shake. It's just a love for an animal and the thrill of racing them.

HÉLÈNE BERGERON

ACADIAN PERFORMER

For me to learn dancing when I was young, it was as natural as learning to walk, because it was just a part of our growing up. But I wasn't learning to dance, to do it in public. Like Dad, he played the fiddle not to be in the spotlight or to be on stage, but because it was a part of him.

My father played the fiddle every day that I grew up. That was his escape, his way of relaxing. He had put in long days fishing. He would come home and just sit with his fiddle in his room and play and play and play. And his fiddle hero was Winston "Scotty" Fitzgerald. I can remember each tune on Winston's records because I heard them so much when I was growing up.

I started around eight and I used to go to all the step dancing contests because my father would go and play at all these contests. I can remember going to tiny little communities and old little one-room schools with the little potbellied stove in the middle of the floor. And the judges were just sort of picked off the street.

I remember wonderful parties at my grandparents', my father's parents. They lived just across the road from us. All my aunts and uncles and my grandparents, and our family and my aunts' and uncles' families — all those kids, we would all be at my grandparents'. And the music was going in the kitchen and they'd bring in a board, you know a piece of wood, to dance on. And all the kids would be sitting on the stairs watching what was going on in the kitchen 'cause there wasn't enough room in the kitchen for everybody. I can still picture my grandfather dancing. He was a short little man. His arms were flying and his feet were flying. Everything was just done with so much abandon. They'd break out in a few songs and then the fiddling would start again and one of the kids would be told to go and do a step.

OPPOSITE: *Hélène's father, Eddie Arsenault*

82

There weren't as many kids then playing the fiddle as now. As a matter of fact, I had never seen a young person playing the fiddle when I was growing up. That's why it never occurred to me to pick it up. And I had also never seen a woman play the fiddle. To me it was an older man's instrument. It never, ever, entered my mind to give it a try then. And that's my one big regret now, that I didn't start when I was young. But it just wasn't a kid's instrument, and it certainly wasn't a girl's instrument.

"Then the fiddling would start again."

When I was thirteen I stopped altogether. It was not "cool" to step dance.

I moved back to P.E.I. when I was twenty-eight, I think. I was asked to dance in a step dancing contest because they didn't have enough adults registered. I thought it was the biggest joke, and then I thought, well, why not. So I dusted off a few of my old steps and I went and I won first place. Well, that opened a whole door — I was rediscovering my roots. After that I just got more and more hooked on the whole traditional thing. I was just also realizing what a good fiddler my father was. Because I was so used to hearing him play when I grew up and not hearing very many other fiddlers. I didn't realize how good he was until I actually tried to start playing myself.

Hélène Bergeron

I see a lot of people of my generation who grew up in musical families and who play music. Their kids are picking it up too. My kids have it in their blood. They both learned to dance without any tutoring from me. It's wonderful to see it passed on to each generation. My father had no notions of teaching us how to dance or play the fiddle or anything like that. It just got soaked into our systems and it's coming out now.

◆ ◆ ◆ ◆ ◆ ◆ ◆ ◆ ◆ ◆ ◆ ◆ ◆

KEVIN CHAISSON

MUSICIAN

I guess it [fiddling] goes back five or six generations that we know of for sure. It was always the fiddle. My two brothers are real good players and a couple of my sisters have some fun with it. All my family all sing, they all dance, some of them play the piano.

When we were young, especially in the wintertime, if there was a storm forecasted you could see the headlights heading for our place. To get stormstayed at Mom and Dad's, that was the idea of the thing. It was music all night. It was nothing professional, but we just had a circus. We had a great time.

We used to have a band, my brothers and I. We were into the country music and the old time. Before we went to a dance I used to go out to Kenny's place and we'd play for half an hour or more — fiddle. And when we were done playing, it was just like you were revitalized. That's the kind

Kevin Chaisson (foreground) with brother Peter

of effect it has on me. Like when I hear a nice slow air, it just puts the shivers right through me. It's hard to explain, it's just the nicest feeling. I also think that it runs from generation to generation. I'm sure it ran in my father's veins and it runs in my veins too, and his father before him. With the fiddle it's feeling.

The fiddle got a bad name a generation before. Even my grandfather across the road here, he didn't want my father to play the fiddle. Because, he said, "I don't want you to see as many sunrises as I did." That was his way of saying I don't want you out playing the fiddle. But it didn't work.

Years ago, the fiddler and the rum went hand in hand. If you wanted to have a few tunes or have a party you called the fiddler. He was the next thing to the parish priest. But it's a complete turnaround now. It's very rare that you'll see a fiddler out playing half-cut, or drunk. It just don't happen any more. In that respect too, it's gained a little more respect.

"To get stormstayed at Mom and Dad's, that was the idea."

"Shoulder to shoulder."

When we were kids, my father played fiddle a lot. My father was employed building bridges and wharves and all that stuff. So in the wintertime he was around home. And he loved the fiddle and he played until his heart's content. Whether he was aware of it, or whether we were aware of it, the music was there and we were absorbing the music all the time. My father's dead twelve years now, and I can still see Dad sitting at the end of the table playing the fiddle. That's one of the best memories I had.

My father started the [Rollo Bay] fiddle festival out here in 1975. There were no kids playing fiddle then. Between that time period and this, there has been a lot of ground gained with the fiddle, definitely. You got kids playing fiddle all over the place. You go down to see the ceilidhs down at Montecello — kids are in there dancing square sets. That stuff wasn't to be had years ago. In order for it to happen in places like that, in halls, it has to happen in homes. Definitely, there's an upswing in traditional music.

It's picking up momentum all the time. And I hope it grows and grows. I hope there's an acre of fiddlers before the day I die, shoulder to shoulder.

❖ ❖ ❖ ❖ ❖ ❖ ❖

IMAGES

I was fishing for sixty-four, sixty-five years. It was an independent life, you were your own boss. If I was a young man today, I'd go back to sea again.

CLIVE BRUCE

I started in an open boat, a stick for steering. And a gas engine and a truck transmission, and an old capstan for a trap hauler. My sounder was a lead of twine, a reel that you dropped down, and a compass. That was all the navigation equipment that you had, and you made do with that.

WALTER BRUCE

I love farmers as a group of people. I just have tremendous compassion for them.

ISABEL CAMPBELL

I think it's a really good place to bring up children, on the farm. The family is closer, there is no doubt about that.

EDITH LING

The rate of farm abandonment is nothing like it was a generation ago, but the number of farms in P.E.I. continues to decline. It doesn't mean necessarily that every time you lose a farm you lose all that farmland, but generally you lose some of it. So the changes continue.

IAN MACQUARRIE

If you have any eyes whatsoever, you cannot but be totally fascinated by what is going on here. I find actually that you have to rest your eyes here. It's like the experience that you have of going into many, many galleries in one day. There's so much visual information. For artists it's wonderful.

HILDA WOOLNOUGH

I see beauty — beauty everywhere I look.

RUTH PAYNTER

When I hear a nice slow air, it just puts the shivers right through me. It's hard to explain, it's just the nicest feeling. I also think that it runs from generation to generation. I'm sure it ran in my father's veins and it runs in my veins too, and his father before him. With the fiddle it's feeling.

KEVIN CHAISSON

My father had no notions of teaching us how to dance or play the fiddle or anything like that. It just got soaked into our systems and it's coming out now.

HÉLÈNE BERGERON

I hope there's an acre of fiddlers before the day I die, shoulder to shoulder.

KEVIN CHAISSON

For more photos, products and information about the author and journey:
www.larryjacobsonauthor.com

The author welcomes comments and questions at:
larry@larryjacobsonauthor.com

Published by:

Buoy Press
Emeryville, California
www.buoypress.com
sales@buoypress.com

Ordering information:
Orders by U.S. trade bookstores and wholesalers, please contact:
sales@buoypress.com

ISBN: 978-0-9828-787-9-8
Library of Congress Control Number: 2010913404

Book design and production by Joel Friedlander
www.TheBookDesigner.com

World map by Rachel Arends

Printed in the United States of America

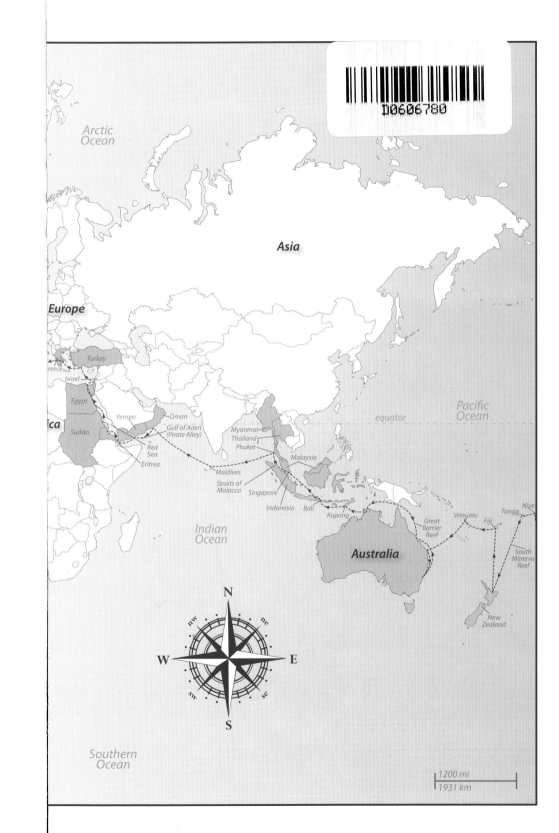

To Roger,
Thank you for
you support. May
all your dreams come
true!

Larry Jacobson

The Boy Behind the Gate

How His Dream of Sailing Around the World
Became a Six-Year Odyssey of Adventure, Fear,
Discovery, and Love

LARRY JACOBSON

BUOY PRESS / EMERYVILLE

Dedication

To my mother, Julia. Through demonstration, she has given
me the courage and strength to fulfill my dreams.
To my father, Abe. If only you could see me now with a
wrench in my hand.
And to Al Joyce, who gave the best advice of all:
"Go, man! Go!"

Acknowledgments

Many people assisted in helping make this book a reality. I'd like to thank those people here.

Bill Claypool, for tirelessly reading the manuscript and giving feedback in such a way that kept me buoyed, rather than sinking.

Jake Jacobson, for his expert legal advice.

Bob Joyce, for helping me through the struggles of publishing a book and for motivating me to keep going through my moments of doubt.

Bill McDonald, for his continued interest in my adventures and for his support and encouragement of the book.

Ken Smith, for sticking by me while living with a writer who sometimes seemed to be going cuckoo and for recognizing that talking to myself was part of the process. For his tireless tutoring of Word and keeping my computer up and running.

John van Duyl, for editing and rescuing the manuscript, encouraging me to let go, and for raising my writing standards.

Patrik, John, Lynette, Brad, Laura, Biagio, Clark, Dan, Karen, Mike, and our other cruising friends, for reminding me of events that may have slipped through the cracks.

And to the countless friends who kept up the encouragement with expressions, such as "Can't wait to read it!" and "When is that damn book coming out?!"

To Live on the Edge

I have stood at the edge
Of the oceans.
I have stared in awe
At the power before me,
That pulled and tugged,
Until there was only the sea.
I left my life behind
To become a wanderer.
To explore, to live on the edge,
To search for something.
For that one thing that could satisfy
The urge that comes over me,
To keep moving, to wonder, to see.
I have circled the globe,
Sailed the seas,
Stared into death's eye.
Yet still my thirst remains unquenched.
Now I stand on the edge again
Staring at the wind blown waters,
Wondering where I belong.
Do I go or do I stay.
I ask it of myself
Each and every day.

Larry Jacobson, 2009